P9-ARB-031

Our Basic FREEDOMS

FREEDOM of ASSEMBLY

KELLY WITTMANN

Gareth Stevens
PUBLISHING

Please visit our website, www.garethstevens.com.
For a free color catalog of all our high-quality books,
call toll free 1-800-542-2595 or fax 1-877-542-2596.

Cataloging-in-Publication Data

Names: Wittmann, Kelly.
Title: Freedom of assembly / Kelly Wittmann.
Description: New York : Gareth Stevens Publishing, 2017. | Series: Our basic freedoms | Includes index.
Identifiers: ISBN 9781482461046 (pbk.) | ISBN 9781482461824 (library bound) | ISBN 9781482461053 (6 pack)
Subjects: LCSH: Assembly, Right of--United States--History--Juvenile literature. | Assembly, Right of--United
  States--Juvenile literature.
Classification: LCC KF4778.W57 2017 | DDC 323.4'8--dc23

Published in 2017 by
Gareth Stevens Publishing
111 East 14th Street, Suite 349
New York, NY 10003

Developed and Produced by Focus Strategic Communications, Inc.
Project Manager: Adrianna Edwards
Editor: Ron Edwards
Layout and Composition: Ruth Dwight
Copyeditors: Adrianna Edwards, Francine Geraci
Media Researchers: Maria DeCambra, Adrianna Edwards
Proofreader: Francine Geraci
Index: Ron Edwards

Photo Credits: Credit Abbreviations: I iStockLOC Library of Congress; NARA National Archives and
Records Administration; S Shutterstock; WC Wikimedia Commons. Position on the page: T: top, C: center,
B: bottom, L: left, R: right. Cover: Andrew Rich/I, 4: Everett - Art/S; 5: Jjmusgrover/WC; 6: Cheryl Casey/S;
7: ChameleonsEye/S; 8: Everett Historical/S; 9: JPL Designs/S; 10: WC; 11: Daderot/WC; 12: Lukas Maverick
Greyson/S; 13: 1000 Words/S; 14: NARA/532892; 15: BPL/WC; 16: StacieStauffSmith Photos/S; 17: Hafakot/S;
18: jiawangkun/S; 20: Everett Historical/S; 21: Everett Historical/S; 23: John F. Kennedy Presidential Library
and Museum/JFKWHP-KN-18351; 24: LOC/LC-DIG-ppmsca-24360; 25: NARA/542015; 27: NARA/ 306-PSD-65-
1882 (Box 93); 28: NARA/542069; 29: LOC/LC-UXZ6-1847; 30: Everett Collection/S; 31: United States Holocaust
Memorial Museum, courtesy of Belarusian State Archive of Documentary Film and Photography/PA14532; 32:
Eddau/WC; 33: Svieta Imnadze/S; 34: Lawrence Samuels/WC; 35: Joseph Sohm/S; 36: Paul Prescott/S; 37 T:
LOC/LC-B201-3643-12; 37 B: MariaSW/S; 38: Samuel Perry/S; 39: Dubova/S; 40: 360b/S; 41: MidoSemsem/S;
42: Focus Strategic Communications, Inc.; 43: Stuart Miles/S; 44: a katz/S; 45: Wavebreakmedia/S.

Printed in the United States of America
CPSIA compliance information: Batch CW17GS: For further information contact
Gareth Stevens, New York, New York at 1-800-542-2595.

CONTENTS

CHAPTER 1
COLLECTIVE
CONCERNS

YOUTHFUL VOICE

Long before James Madison wrote the 10 amendments that became known as the Bill of Rights (1791), and well before he was the fourth president of the United States (1809–1817), he was a young man intent on leaving his mark on the political landscape. Our freedom to assemble is owed in large part to his brilliant thinking and hard work.

DRIVING AMBITION

Just 25 years old when America declared its independence from England in 1776, James Madison had graduated from Princeton University in 1771. He came from a wealthy, land- and slave-owning Virginia family. During the Revolutionary War, he was a member of the Virginia state legislature, and he studied the words and actions of his mentor and fellow future president, Thomas Jefferson. Though young Madison was not a religious man, he believed strongly that people should have the right to assemble to practice the religion of their choice, even if that was no religion at all.

Madison (1751–1836) came from one of Virginia's leading families, many of whom became very wealthy from planting tobacco for trade.

FREEDOM OF ASSEMBLY AND RELIGION

In the pre-Revolutionary colonies, anyone who wanted to set up a church, or even just preach to a group of people in the street, had to obtain a license from the established Anglican Church. The Anglican Church was recognized as the official church of the state, but Madison and many other proponents of the freedom of assembly felt that was wrong. They believed that any religious group had the right to assemble to worship together, whether the established church or the government liked it or not. This concern led Madison to help Thomas Jefferson in drafting the Virginia **Statute** for Religious Freedom in 1777. For the very first time in America, freedom of religion for all religious groups, including Catholics and Jews, was guaranteed.

CHURCH ASSEMBLIES

The laws of Virginia compelled its citizens to gather and worship at state-sanctioned Anglican churches (such as St. Peter's Church in New Kent County in Virginia, pictured here) and to support them through taxation. Our Founding Fathers did not think that was right. They thought that people should support their churches voluntarily, through **tithing.**

ASSEMBLY RIGHTS FOR ALL

After the United States declared independence and defeated the British forces, it was time to craft the laws of the new United States of America. Madison went to work in the House of Representatives. He wanted all Americans, not just Virginians, to have the right of assembly. That is one of the reasons why, in 1789, he wrote the Bill of Rights. In the First Amendment of that bill, the freedom of assembly is guaranteed:

"Congress shall make no law respecting an establishment of religion, or prohibiting the free exercise thereof; or abridging the freedom of speech, or of the press; or the right of the people peaceably to assemble, and to petition the government for a redress of grievances."

The First Amendment of the Bill of Rights guaranteed the freedom of assembly.

ASSEMBLY BEYOND RELIGION

With these words, Madison moved beyond religious freedom to assert the right of groups of people to assemble for any reason. They might want to worship. They might want to form a new political party. They might want to protest a government action. They might just want to "hang out" and talk about anything. The point was that as long as they were doing so peacefully and legally, they did not **infringe** on the rights of others, and they should be left alone by the government. It was not the government's business to tell citizens how or when they could get together.

James Madison and many other Americans felt this right should have been included in the Constitution, so why was it not? Why was it necessary to write the Bill of Rights later?

Fast Fact

THE BAPTIST INFLUENCE

Though Presbyterians and Methodists also went against the Anglican grain in colonial America, it was probably the Baptist movement that had the most effect on laws relating to the freedom of assembly in America. The

Baptists wanted to spread their beliefs in **biblical literalism** and adult baptism, but the Anglican Church was threatened by those ideas and tried to curtail their right to assemble. Today, adult baptism is still practiced around the world.

CHAPTER 2

GROUNDED IN GRIEVANCES

REJECTION OF RIGHTS

At the Constitutional Convention in Philadelphia in 1787, Virginia delegate George Mason proposed a Bill of Rights. However, it was unanimously rejected. Why? And what did Mason and his like-minded allies do about it?

CLASH OF VIEWS

George Mason was a neighbor of the man who would become our first president, George Washington. Like Washington, he was a landowner and slaveholder and had political ambitions. After months of debate at the Convention, Mason and some other delegates expressed concern that there was to be no bill of rights included in the United States Constitution.

George Mason (1725–1792) has a school named after him—George Mason University—in Fairfax, Virginia, just outside Washington, DC.

ANTI-FEDERALISTS

Mason and some of his colleagues were called **Anti-Federalists** because, although they were working to form a central government, they wanted limits on its power. After their experiences with what they saw as the British abuse of power, they wanted assurances that their new government would not overpower the states and infringe on the liberty of individuals. They wanted to make sure that the Executive branch (the president and the Cabinet) would not be able to dictate to the Legislative branch (the House and the Senate). The third branch, the Judicial, was designed to balance the other two.

THE THREE BRANCHES OF GOVERNMENT

LEGISLATIVE
(makes laws)

EXECUTIVE
(carries out laws)

JUDICIAL
(evaluates laws)

SOUTHERN SLAVE OWNER

As a southern planter, George Mason was also worried that the northern states would have too much say in how southerners should live their lives. And even though he publicly called for an end to the slave trade, he remained a slave owner who wanted to protect his livelihood and his property.

Fast Fact
FREEING THE SLAVES

George Washington instructed that his slaves be freed after his wife's death, but George Mason did not follow suit. His will left his slaves in bondage, dividing them among his children. Freed slaves were sometimes able to prosper (as depicted in this painting), but none of them enjoyed rights such as the freedom of assembly. They were strictly monitored by authorities for any sign of political organizing.

SIGNING THE CONSTITUTION

One of the important rights that Mason and his **cohorts** wanted to secure in a bill of rights was the right of assembly, which protected those who would protest government actions they disagreed with. When those at the Constitutional Convention declined to add a bill of rights to the Constitution, Mason and delegates Elbridge Gerry and Edmund Randolph exercised this right when they banded together and refused to sign the Constitution. However, 39 other delegates did sign. Many of them were exhausted after months of debate and hard work in often hot weather, and they just wanted to go home.

The Constitution was finally signed on September 17, 1787.

EVENTUAL COMPROMISE

The game was on between the Federalists and the Anti-Federalists. Both groups used the press and their own publications to put forth their cases. The Federalists urged American citizens to **lobby** their representatives to sign the Constitution as it was. The Anti-Federalists pressured those same Americans to beware of a Constitution that did not include a bill of rights. James Madison knew that Mason and the other Anti-Federalists would not be satisfied until some kind of compromise was made. So he drafted the Bill of Rights, including the First Amendment, which guaranteed "the right of the people peaceably to assemble…."

A large crowd gathered on July 14, 2013, in New York City to peacefully protest the Trayvon Martin murder case.

IMPORTANCE OF ASSEMBLY RIGHTS

Why was freedom of assembly so important to George Mason and the other delegates who refused to sign the Constitution? One reason was that many people had fled Britain and Europe and came to America because (among other things) they had no right of assembly in their native countries. They could not assemble to change the political process without harassment from the authorities. They could not assemble and worship as they pleased without drawing fire from the powerful Anglican and Roman Catholic Churches. Often, even completely innocent gatherings having nothing to do with politics or religion were looked upon with needless suspicion.

Protesters clash with police in London, England, during a large rally on March 26, 2011.

ASSEMBLING FOR REVOLUTION

In addition to the lack of rights in Britain and Europe, the Founding Fathers knew that without the right to assembly and collective action, the Revolution would not have happened. Perhaps the most famous example of colonists assembling to protest the unfair rule of the Crown was the Boston Tea Party. On December 16, 1773, protesters, dressed up as Native Americans, boarded three East India Company ships in Boston Harbor and threw an entire shipment of tea overboard. They asserted that King George's tax on tea was an example of taxation without representation. The colonists did not have representatives in the British Parliament, so they felt they owed no taxes to the British Crown.

Some criticized the Boston Tea Party as a violent mob scene (even though no lives were lost), but others defended it as a legitimate act of protest.

Fast Fact

TEA OR COFFEE?

In colonial America, tea drinking was all the rage. After the Boston Tea Party, however, tea drinking came to be seen as an unpatriotic act, so many Americans turned to coffee. To this day, coffee is three times more popular in the United States than tea is.

THE RIGHT TO ASSEMBLY—NOT FOR EVERYONE

Although they did not condone illegal acts such as the Boston Tea Party, the delegates to the Constitutional Convention wanted to protect the right of the people to assemble and stage legal demonstrations. Protest had been the life's blood of the American Revolution. The delegates were not about to give up the right to assemble without a fight. Of course, when they spoke of the right to assemble, the Founding Fathers were speaking only about white men who owned land. African Americans, Native Americans, women, and other minorities certainly could not just gather in the street or in a meeting house and plot revolution. The men who wrote the First Amendment had no intention of changing that!

Green Dragon Tavern, Union Street.

GREEN DRAGON TAVERN

Boston revolutionaries, including the famous silversmith Paul Revere, often got together at the Green Dragon Tavern to secretly plot against the British. The building, which historians call "the Headquarters of the Revolution," was torn down in 1854.

CHAPTER 3

ASSEMBLY—NOT ALWAYS PEACEFUL

THE RIGHT TO READ

Practically speaking, the Bill of Rights had little impact on most Americans for many years. Though Americans said they supported such rights, it took a long time for them to understand how they would be applied in the courts of law. In 1870, 20 percent of the total population was still **illiterate**, and among African Americans and other minorities, nearly 80 percent could not read or write. When people cannot read, they cannot learn about the legal system. They have no way of finding out the rights to which they are entitled. Illiteracy made public assembly very difficult because if you cannot even write or read a poster announcing a meeting, how will you publicize that meeting or know to attend? If you cannot communicate over long distances by letter, how will you gather like-minded people together? If you cannot hand out pamphlets at the end of a meeting, how will word spread of your ideas?

Illiteracy is a way of controlling people.

STOP ILLITERACY NOW!

LACK OF UNDERSTANDING

In the 1700s and early 1800s, even literate Americans were not very interested in using their skills to organize protests. They were weary after the Revolutionary War and were eager for some peace. "Troublemakers" who stirred up collective action were often dealt with harshly by legal authorities, and this usually caused little controversy. Despite the fact that the Bill of Rights existed, the American public did not yet fully understand the concept of individual civil liberties.

Today, the idea of individual civil liberties, or **civil rights**, is engrained in the minds of most Americans.

A DIFFERENT KIND OF REVOLUTION

Between 1760 and 1840, another revolution happened—but it was not the kind that involved wars and weapons. Machines were invented and slowly began to replace hand tools. This was called the **Industrial Revolution**. Products could now be made much faster and more efficiently, and the owners of those businesses could become very wealthy very quickly. However, in most cases, they did not want to share that wealth with their workers.

Fast Fact

FLAUNTING WEALTH

When the early titans of business flaunted their wealth by building palatial homes (like the Vanderbilt family's summer home, The Breakers, shown here), it often made workers more determined to assemble and fight for better working conditions.

WORKER UNREST

At first, workers put up little fight because they believed that the poor could never challenge the wealthy and win. But slowly, that mind-set began to change. When it did, the right to assemble became important to a large proportion of the American population.

Workers were dissatisfied in this new kind of workplace. Not only did most of them earn very little money, but the factories were often unhealthy or even dangerous places. Men, women, and children worked long hours in these places, and there were no laws to protect them.

As traditional artisans were replaced by assembly-line manufacturing and unskilled workers became the majority, wages and working conditions worsened. When workers assembled to ask for more money or safer working conditions, they were often arrested and charged with criminal conspiracy.

By the mid-1800s, modern labor unions began to appear. One of the first national labor organizations was the Knights of Labor. Founded in 1869, the Knights coordinated thousands of strikes across the nation until they disbanded in the 1880s. The modern American labor movement dates from that time. The American Federation of Labor (AFL) was founded in 1881 and oversaw 37,000 strikes over the next two decades.

FACTORY WORKING CONDITIONS

In the years following the Civil War, American industry grew extremely rapidly. Factories sprang up everywhere, but there were few laws regarding workplace safety or worker rights. Workers often labored long hours for little pay and in terrible conditions. To save money, owners ignored dangerous conditions. Sometimes tragedy resulted.

Fast Fact

★ ★ ★

THE TRIANGLE SHIRTWAIST FACTORY FIRE

On March 25, 1911, in New York City, the Triangle Shirtwaist Factory fire became one of the deadliest industrial disasters in US history. The fire destroyed the factory (shown here) and killed 146 garment workers—women and girls—largely because safety measures were ignored. The tragedy focused public attention on factory working conditions and led to the passage of safety laws and regulations. Americans began to take a kinder view of the right to assemble and collectively protest. As a result of that shift in public opinion, unions became stronger.

LABOR ORGANIZING

Workers realized that the only way they could take on owners was to organize and protest. In order to do that, they had to use their right to assemble. Individual workers had little to no power compared to owners, and if they asked for more money, they were often fired and replaced. Workers soon discovered that if they banded together and refused to work until conditions improved, they could make real change. It was a difficult process, but after they formed unions and began lobbying lawmakers, American workers saw labor conditions improve.

Fast Fact

ALEXANDER BERKMAN

The vast majority of disgruntled American workers were peaceful protesters, but there were times when anger led to violence. Enraged by the Carnegie Steel Company's refusal to negotiate with the Amalgamated Association of Iron and Steel Workers in 1892, **anarchist** Alexander Berkman (shown here on the right) shot Carnegie chairman Henry Clay Frick. Frick survived, and Berkman's assassination attempt was denounced by the union. Berkman was arrested and served 14 years in prison for attempted murder.

USING THE COURT SYSTEM

In the 1900s, protesters took their cue from the workers who had gone before them. In addition to trying to influence lawmakers—the Legislative branch of government—they began to use the court system to protect their right to assemble. One memorable decision took place in 1937 when the US Supreme Court upheld the right of Dirk De Jonge to speak at a peaceful meeting of the Communist Party in Oregon (*De Jonge v. Oregon*). This was controversial because many communists advocated violent revolution against the US government and America's **capitalist** system. But the Court ruled that an individual's rights to free assembly and freedom of speech were even more important than any damage a political party might do.

Fast Fact

JOSEPH ZACK KORNFEDER

Joseph Zack Kornfeder (1893–1963), also known as Joe Zack, was a founder of the Communist Party of America in 1919. He was sent to South America to organize labor unions and communist parties in Colombia and Venezuela. He was jailed there, but the US State Department gained his release. He returned to the United States and turned anti-communist in 1934. He died in Washington, DC, in 1963.

NAACP

In the early 1900s, African Americans began to exercise their right to assemble. The NAACP—National Association for the Advancement of Colored People—was formed in 1909 by W. E. B. Du Bois and others "to ensure the political, educational, social, and economic equality of rights for all persons and to eliminate racial hatred and racial discrimination." It now has a membership of 300,000 people.

In 1958, the US Supreme Court ruled that the State of Alabama could not demand the NAACP's membership list (*National Association for the Advancement of Colored People v. Alabama*). Many of the people who governed Alabama were fearful of what would happen if African Americans were able to exercise their right of assembly. They wanted the NAACP's list so that they could monitor, and even harass, those who were fighting for civil rights. The Court's ruling was a huge victory for all progressive groups who worked to change the course of history in America. Both the *De Jonge* and the *NAACP* cases set the tone for what was to come in the latter half of the twentieth century.

President John F. Kennedy meets with representatives from the NAACP on July 12, 1961.

CHAPTER 4

TIMES OF TROUBLE

ACTION FOR CHANGE

By the mid-1900s, many Americans had become more open and tolerant. They were more willing to join with others to take action for changes in their society. In the 1960s, college students and "**hippies**" used the right of assembly to protest the Vietnam War. Protests against the Vietnam War became a common sight all over America in the late 1960s and early 1970s. Though many Americans agreed that the war should end, they did not always approve of the protesters' tactics when they assembled, such as when they burned their draft cards. Even after the war ended in 1973, there were bad feelings on all sides for many years.

Students protest the Vietnam War in 1968 outside the White House in Washington, DC.

THE CIVIL RIGHTS MOVEMENT

As more and more women began working outside the home, they used that right to protest unequal treatment. African Americans and other minorities continued to use the nonviolent tactics that had been successful for activists such as Dr. Martin Luther King Jr. But these exercises of the right of assembly came with a price.

The cases being heard by the courts in the 1960s regarding the right of assembly reflected the turbulent times. On March 2, 1961, a group of church leaders and students held a peaceful march in favor of equal civil rights in Columbia, South Carolina. Even though the marchers had done nothing violent, police arrested 187 of them. They were convicted of the crime of breach of the peace. However, in 1963, they were cleared of blame when the US Supreme Court ruled that the state had disregarded their right of assembly. The Court expressed that the state could not outlaw "the peaceful expression of unpopular views."

Dr. Martin Luther King Jr. led the Civil Rights March on Washington, DC, on August 28, 1963, to promote equality for African Americans.

DISCRIMINATION AND SEGREGATION

African Americans have suffered discrimination, harassment, and worse, especially in the US South. The Civil War (1861–1865) was fought largely over the issue of slavery: the South wanted to retain it, and the North wanted to abolish it. Eleven southern states that formed the Confederacy were eventually defeated by the Union forces of the North. All slaves were declared free on January 1, 1863, when Abraham Lincoln issued the Emancipation Proclamation. The period known as Reconstruction (1865–1877) was supposed to usher in an era of citizenship and equality for 4 million freed slaves. But it was not successful.

Throughout the South, governments refused to cooperate. They systematically discriminated against African Americans through racial segregation and voter fraud in a series of laws known as the Jim Crow laws. In extreme cases, the Ku Klux Klan terrorized blacks through intimidation and violence, lynching being the most extreme. In the late 1800s and early 1900s, nearly 5,000 people were lynched, three-quarters of whom were African Americans.

ADVANCES IN CIVIL RIGHTS

It took a long time, but things finally began to change after World War II, which saw many African Americans in the US military. In 1948, President Harry S. Truman desegregated the armed forces. Court cases followed, and the 1950s saw several challenges to racial segregation. A landmark event occurred in 1955 when Rosa Parks refused to give up her seat on a bus to a white man in Montgomery, Alabama. The Montgomery Bus Boycott lasted more than a year but managed to desegregate public transportation. This event marked the beginning of the end for the Jim Crow laws. In 1964, President Lyndon Johnson signed the Civil Rights Act, which outlawed discrimination based on race, color, religion, sex, or national origin.

Rosa Parks is pictured here in 1955 with Dr. Martin Luther King Jr.

CIVIL RIGHTS LEADERS

Foremost among leaders of the Civil Rights Movement was Martin Luther King Jr. (1929–1968). King was a Baptist minister from Georgia who advocated nonviolent civil disobedience to advance the cause of African American equality. He was the leader of the Montgomery Bus Boycott in 1955 as well as the 1963 March on Washington, DC. It was during the latter that Dr. King delivered his now-famous "I Have a Dream" speech.

THE DREAM SPEECH: SOME HIGHLIGHTS

"I have a dream that my four little children will one day live in a nation where they will not be judged by the color of their skin but by the content of their character … And when this happens, when we allow freedom to ring … we will be able to speed up that day when all of God's children, black men and white men, Jews and Gentiles, Protestants and Catholics, will be able to join hands and sing in the words of the old Negro spiritual: 'Free at last! Free at last! Thank God Almighty, we are free at last!'"

Dr. Martin Luther King Jr. gives his "I Have a Dream" speech on August 28, 1963.

MARTIN LUTHER KING'S LEGACY

King was awarded the Nobel Peace Prize in 1964 for his contributions to nonviolent resistance to racial injustice in the United States. Tragically, he was assassinated on April 4, 1968, in Memphis, Tennessee. Shocked and frustrated African Americans followed news of the assassination, and riots broke out across the nation.

MALCOLM X

Not all black leaders believed in King's nonviolent resistance. For example, Malcolm X was an advocate of black self-defense and black self-determination. He rejected integration and the entire Civil Rights Movement, and called for the separation of black and white Americans. In 1965, he was killed by the Nation of Islam, a black separatist group.

Malcolm X (right) met with Martin Luther King Jr. in 1964 to hear the Senate debate on the Civil Rights Act. It was the only time the two men ever met.

OTHER BLACK MOVEMENTS

Other leaders stepped up to try and fill Martin Luther King Jr.'s shoes. Some, such as the Black Power leaders, called for armed self-defense. The Black Panthers advocated violent revolution. No one of King's stature emerged, but other leaders—such as Louis Farrakhan, Stokely Carmichael, Jesse Jackson, and Al Sharpton—became prominent.

None of the civil rights leaders of the 1960s could ever have predicted the outcome of the election of 2008. Americans elected their first black president, Barack Obama. Still, racial tensions were never far below the surface of US public life.

Barack Obama gives a speech on January 6, 2008, during his presidential campaign.

THE SKOKIE MARCH

One of the most controversial cases involving the freedom of assembly was *National Socialist Party of America v. Village of Skokie*. Both the Supreme Court of Illinois and the US Supreme Court heard the case in 1977. The National Socialists were the American branch of the group better known as the Nazis, who had terrorized much of Europe in the 1930s and 1940s. During those years, the Nazis murdered millions of people, including over 6 million Jews, in what is now called the **Holocaust**. Many of those who survived did so because they moved to America to find peace and safety.

These child survivors of the Holocaust were photographed at the Auschwitz concentration camp in 1945.

SUPREME COURT RULING

In 1977, there were over 40,000 Jewish people living in the Chicago suburb of Skokie, Illinois. When the National Socialist Party announced that they wanted to hold a march in Skokie, the Jewish citizens were hurt and angry. They did not think the Nazis should be allowed to parade through their neighborhoods and make a mockery of their suffering. Many agreed, and the Illinois state courts issued an order to stop the march. However, the US Supreme Court ruled that the Nazis were free to assemble and march legally in Skokie. In the end, the Nazis chose to march in Chicago instead, but they had won the case.

Fast Fact

ILLINOIS HOLOCAUST MUSEUM & EDUCATION CENTER

In 1978, local Holocaust survivors set up a foundation in Skokie, Illinois, to combat hatred and racism. In 2009, the foundation became the Illinois Holocaust Museum & Education Center. It is dedicated to "preserving the legacy of the Holocaust by honoring the memories of those who were lost."

PRIVATE VERSUS PUBLIC

In the 1960s, citizens were sometimes confused as to whether shopping malls were public or private property and what that meant as far as their right to assemble. The Supreme Court ruled that malls had the right to set their own rules—except in "company towns" where there was no public alternative for assembly.

The Supreme Court did not always rule in favor of protesters, however. In 1968, Lloyd Center was a large, privately owned shopping center in Portland, Oregon. The mall did not allow people to hand out pamphlets of any kind, but they did allow some charitable organizations, such as the American Legion and the Salvation Army, to collect donations there. Political candidates from both the Republican and Democratic parties were permitted to speak there, too. Gun-carrying police officers, rather than private security guards, kept the peace and enforced the center's rules.

When the Lloyd Center Mall opened in 1960, it was the largest mall in America. It even had a skating rink.

DRAFT PROTESTERS

Activists protesting the Vietnam War tested those private–public rules on November 14, 1968, by handing out pamphlets at the Lloyd Center condemning the military draft. Though the protest was peaceful, a customer complained to the police. The activists were removed from the mall. A district court sided with the protesters in ruling that their First Amendment rights had been violated, but the Supreme Court did not agree. On June 22, 1972, a majority of the justices said that since there were plenty of public places in Portland where the activists could have handed out their pamphlets, they did not have a right to do so on private property.

Students burn draft cards at a rally at California State University, Fullerton, in May 1979 to protest Congress's attempt to reinstate conscription.

CHAPTER 5

YOUTH AND ASSEMBLY

IMPACT ON KIDS

Though all American liberties have an impact on kids, freedom of assembly has had a unique impact on younger generations throughout history.

FROM THE BEGINNING

Young Americans have been affected by the freedom to assemble since even before our country was founded. Thousands of children and teens fled with their families to the New World because their right to assemble was not upheld in their native countries in Great Britain and Europe. The kids who lived through the American Revolution, our nation's first great collective action, learned firsthand how important the right to assemble was—as their descendants would one day discover for themselves.

Fast Fact

MAYFLOWER CHILDREN

Of the 102 passengers on the *Mayflower*—the ship that sailed from England to America in 1620—31 were children. The people of the *Mayflower* left England specifically because they were not allowed to assemble there to practice their Puritan religion.

SWEATSHOPS

As the simple manner of colonial living gave way to modern times, young Americans did not passively sit by while others used the right to assemble in order to effect change. Instead, children and teenagers who worked in the sweatshops of the Industrial Revolution joined their parents at workers' meetings.

Today, in this era of globalization, we find that more and more of our favorite consumer goods are made overseas, often in countries that use child labor. Some companies in Asia and elsewhere exploit child workers to produce goods for Adidas, Nike, Disney, and most sports leagues. In 1996, it was revealed that Kathie Lee Gifford's and Wal-Mart's clothing were produced by children in Central America and elsewhere.

Many children work long hours in workshops like this textile factory in Delhi, India.

ASSEMBLY RIGHTS FOR OTHERS

Just as African American, Native American, and Latino people marched demanding their rights in the civil rights era, another group used the power of assembly to demand fairness and equality. Dating back to the 1800s, suffragists demanded the vote for women. A few countries, such as New Zealand and parts of Australia, complied in the 1890s. Several European nations followed, and the United States passed the Nineteenth Amendment, which gave women the vote in 1920.

It took a great many suffragist marches, like this one in New York City in 1913, to win women the right to vote.

Feminists hold a political rally in Sweden in 2016.

Since then, women have played leading roles in demanding rights beyond suffrage. The feminist movement has used the freedom of assembly to advocate many important issues having to do with equality and civil rights.

CAMPUS ACTIVISM

Many Americans have their first experience in exercising the freedom of assembly while in school. Though schools have always held elections for their official student governments, today students are free to make their opinions known through social media. However, elementary and high school students are legal minors, and, as such, do not have as much influence as college students.

Once in college, and having reached adulthood, students feel they have the right to assemble over just about anything. These days, many students believe that if they are paying such high tuitions to these institutions, they deserve to have a voice. Most of the issues they assemble over are very serious, like racism on campus or the university's investment in corporations that are ethically questionable.

There seems to be a resurgence of campus activism in America. Whether over vital issues or less serious concerns—such as football coaching and cafeteria food—students are assembling and making their opinions known.

Student protesters in Chicago in 2010 use their freedom of assembly to demonstrate against US military involvement in Iraq and Afghanistan.

TECH-DRIVEN ASSEMBLY

In this age of Internet technology, young people are more connected than ever and will continue to exercise their right to the freedom of assembly. Many youths are coming together out of their concern that student loans, and the debt they cause, have gotten out of hand. They worry about their futures in higher education, but also in the military. Interest in foreign policy is high, as it is mostly young people who must fight in the wars that older people start. Today's young people would rather use their freedom to assemble to effect positive change than to have to use it to protest another war.

Fast Fact

TECHNOLOGY AND ASSEMBLIES

Computer technology, handheld devices, and Internet access can make it easier to organize assemblies. But they also allow people to tune others out.

ASSEMBLY ACROSS THE WORLD

Beginning in 2010, several countries in the Arab world experienced a wave of demonstrations that swept through North Africa and the Middle East. Starting with Tunisia in December 2010, the movement swept across Libya, Egypt, Syria, and other countries. It was dubbed the "Arab Spring" because many saw it as a renewal and awakening in the Arab world. What made it different from previous attempts to assemble for change in the Middle East was the participants' use of digital and social media. They were able to capture disturbing images on their cell phones and send them around the world. They did not have to wait for the establishment press to get their message out.

Hosni Mubarak was the fourth president of Egypt, from 1981 until he resigned following massive demonstrations against his corrupt regime in 2011 during the Arab Spring.

REVERSAL OF GAINS

The positive feeling did not last, however, and the protests gave way to civil war and repression. Governments throughout the Middle East used their power to enforce Internet shutdowns, and many of the "netizens" who were involved in the protests were arrested and sometimes even killed. Though people all over the world sympathized, there was little they could do to stop this abuse by the authorities. Several of these countries deteriorated into civil war and chaos, and refugees began flooding out of them, attempting to resettle in Europe. Some people referred to this counterinsurgency as the "Arab Winter."

Egyptians protest in Alexandria in June 2013 during the "Arab Winter."

CHAPTER 6

CONCLUSION

A DELICATE BALANCE

The 10 amendments to the US Constitution, known as the Bill of Rights, were written by James Madison, who had helped draft the Constitution of 1787. Upon reflection, he decided that it did not spell out citizens' rights clearly enough. The idea for the Bill of Rights had originally been proposed by George Mason in 1787 but was voted down. Madison picked it up a couple of years later.

Many Founding Fathers were wary of strong government power after their experiences with British oppression during the Revolutionary period. Yet after suffering a few years under a weak new government, they realized that little could be accomplished without increasing the government's powers. It was a balancing act. In order to strengthen the federal government, they felt the need to spell out citizens' rights so that the central authority would not grow to be too powerful.

The US Constitution and the Declaration of Independence were signed in Philadelphia in what is now called Independence Hall. Today, more than 600,000 people from all over the world visit the site annually.

ASSEMBLY RIGHTS AND THE REVOLUTION

The Founders' experience in the American Revolution led them to understand the importance of citizenship rights, not the least of which was the freedom of assembly. Without that freedom, the Founding Fathers would never have been able to meet and plan American independence. Groups such as the Sons of Liberty were instrumental in defeating the British, and assembly played a central role in those activities.

Of course, protest "rights" were limited to white males, particularly landowners. Other groups—from women to African Americans and Native Americans—were not offered the same rights.

One important type of assembly was association for the purposes of education. The Founders, being highly educated themselves, knew the importance of literacy. But African Americans, women, and other minorities were not encouraged to learn to read, and were sometimes actively discouraged from doing so. Illiteracy meant that groups of minorities were not able to organize to protest their rights.

As late as 1870, 80 percent of African Americans could not read or write, compared to just 20 percent of whites.

CIVIL RIGHTS

By the mid-twentieth century, much of America woke up to the fact that a large minority in their society was being left out: African Americans were not getting their piece of the American Dream and were often treated like second-class citizens. In the South, they were dismissed as inferior and forced to live apart from and defer to white people. The Jim Crow laws enforced segregation on the basis of race.

The entire movement seeking racial equality was known as the Civil Rights Movement. The right of assembly was a central part of that struggle. Martin Luther King Jr. was one of the foremost leaders of the African American quest for equality and acceptance. Despite a half-century of struggle, African Americans have still not achieved full equality. Civil rights protests continue.

Black Lives Matter is an international movement protesting violence against black people. It was founded in 2013. Here, protesters rally in New York City in April 2015.

ASSEMBLING FOR OTHER PROTESTS

In the midst of the civil rights protests came the Vietnam War. College campuses across the United States exploded with protests, demanding everything from voter rights for African Americans to equality for women and the end to the Vietnam War. It was a time of chaos that transformed America and the way we view freedom of assembly.

Today, the protests may not be as widespread or as colorful as those of the 1960s, but freedom of assembly is still central to our society. Now, instead of hand-lettered signs and hippie sit-ins, protesters use social media and modern technology to communicate and arrange details. Still, the aim is unchanged: citizens have to speak up (and assemble) to make their wishes known.

Social media plays an increasing role in our daily lives, and it is transforming the way we exercise our right of assembly.

GLOSSARY

anarchist—a person who promotes revolution against the established power structure

Anti-Federalists—opponents of a centralized federal government

biblical literalism—adherence to the Bible to the exact letter

capitalist—describing an economic system characterized by private ownership and corporations

civil rights—rights guaranteed to all citizens

cohort—a friend or companion

hippies—young people of the 1960s who rejected established institutions and values

Holocaust—the mass slaughter of European Jews by the Nazis in the 1930s and 1940s

illiterate—unable to read and write

Industrial Revolution—the replacement of hand tools with machines in society

infringe—to encroach or trespass

lobby—to try to influence the votes of lawmakers

statute—an enactment made by lawmakers that is defined in a formal document

tithe—a voluntary offering to support a church

FURTHER INFORMATION

Books

Amar, Akhil Reed. *America's Constitution: A Biography*. New York: Random House, 2005.

Gora, Joel M., David Goldberger, Gary M. Stern, and Morton H. Halperin. *The Right to Protest: The Basic ACLU Guide to Free Expression*. Carbondale, IL: Southern Illinois University Press, 1991.

Labunski, Richard. *James Madison and the Struggle for the Bill of Rights*. New York: Oxford University Press, 2006.

Levy, Leonard W. *Origins of the Bill of Rights*. Princeton: Yale University, 1999.

Online

Anglican Church in Virginia
www.history.org/almanack/life/religion/religiondfn.cfm

Atlantic, The, "The Renaissance of Student Activism" by Alia Wong
www.theatlantic.com/education/archive/2015/05/the
-renaissance-of-student-activism/393749

Bill of Rights Institute
billofrightsinstitute.org/educate/educator-resources/landmark
-cases/assembly-and-association

National Archives and Records Administration
www.archives.gov/exhibits/charters/bill_of_rights_transcript.html

National Illiteracy Rates
nces.ed.gov/naal/lit_history.asp

INDEX